CPS-DAVIS/SHIELDS ELEMENTARY

W9-CBM-655

I like music : what can I be?

## DATE DUE

| | | | |
|---|---|---|---|
| | | | |
| | | | |
| | | | |
| | | | |
| | | | |
| | | | |
| | | | |
| | | | |
| | | | |
| | | | |
| | | | |
| | | | |
| | | | |

780
DUB        Dubois, Muriel L.
           I like music : what can I be?

DAVIS/SHIELDS ELEMENTARY SCH
CHICAGO PUBLIC SCHOOLS
4520 SOUTH KEDZIE AVE.
CHICAGO, IL. 60632

# I Like Music

## What Can I Be?

by Muriel L. Dubois

**Consultant:**
Barbara M. Parramore
Professor Emeritus, Curriculum and Instruction
North Carolina State University

Bridgestone Books
an imprint of Capstone Press
Mankato, Minnesota

Bridgestone Books are published by Capstone Press
151 Good Counsel Drive, P.O. Box 669, Mankato, Minnesota 56002
http://www.capstone-press.com

Copyright © 2001 Capstone Press. All rights reserved.
No part of this book may be reproduced without written permission from the publisher.
The publisher takes no responsibility for the use of any of the materials
or methods described in this book, nor for the products thereof.
Printed in the United States of America.

*Library of Congress Cataloging-in-Publication Data*
Dubois, Muriel L.
    I like music: what can I be?/by Muriel L. Dubois.
    p. cm.—(What can I be?)
    Includes bibliographical references and index.
    Summary: Simple text describes various occupations for people who like music and
what they involve, including composer, instrument maker, and recording engineer.
    ISBN 0-7368-0632-6
    1. Music—Vocational guidance—Juvenile literature. [1. Music. 2. Occupations.] I. Title
II. Series.
ML3795 .D9 2001
780'.23—dc21
                00-021250

**Editorial Credits**
Tom Adamson, editor; Heather Kindseth, designer; Katy Kudela, photo researcher

**Photo Credits**
David F. Clobes, 4
David Stover/Pictor, cover, 6
Gregg Andersen, 16
Index Stock Imagery, cover (top inset)
International Stock, cover (bottom inset); Dick Dickinson, 8
Phil Cantor/Pictor, 18
Shaffer Photography/James L. Shaffer, 20
Tom Stodola, 10, 14
Unicorn Stock Photos/R. Baum, cover (middle inset); A. Ramey, 12

1 2 3 4 5 6 06 05 04 03 02 01

# Table of Contents

## People Who Enjoy Music

You might enjoy listening to music. You may like to sing or to play an instrument. Maybe you make up songs. You can have a job working in music when you grow up.

**instrument**
an object that people use to make music

## Composer

Composers make up songs. They write down the musical notes of their songs. Composers may write music for movies or TV shows. Some composers also write lyrics to go with their music.

**lyrics**
the words of a song

## Professional Musician

Professional musicians are paid to play instruments or to sing. They perform for people. Some musicians record music for movies, commercials, or CDs. Professional musicians spend most of their time practicing.

## Music Teacher

Music teachers show students how to read music. They teach students to sing or to play instruments. Some music teachers work with large groups. Others teach small groups or one person at a time.

## Instrument Maker

Instrument makers build musical instruments. They choose materials and follow plans to make instruments. They also may fix instruments. They then play the instruments to make sure they sound as they should.

## Disc Jockey

Disc jockeys play songs on the radio. They play music by many different musicians. They also talk about news and weather between songs. Some disc jockeys play music for parties or weddings.

## Conductor

Conductors lead bands, orchestras, or choirs. They choose music for the group to perform. Conductors rehearse the music with the group. They tell the musicians when to play loud or soft, fast or slow.

**rehearse**
to practice for a public performance

17

## Sound Engineer

Sound engineers record musicians as they perform. Engineers work to make the recorded music sound clear. They remove extra noise from the recording. They also may add special sound effects to recordings or to movie sound tracks.

**sound track**
a recording of music from a movie

## Preparing to Work in Music

You can prepare for a career in music. Listen to different kinds of music. Read books about performers and composers. Learn to read music. Learn to sing or to play an instrument. Join your school choir, band, or orchestra.

# Hands On: Make Rhythm Instruments

All music needs to have an even beat, or rhythm. You can make simple rhythm instruments.

## What You Need

2 empty potato chip tubes with lids
2 sheets of construction paper
Colored markers or crayons
Masking tape
Beads, dried beans, rice, or bird seed

## What You Do

1. Decorate the construction paper with colorful designs.
2. Tape or glue one piece of paper around each tube.
3. Put a few handfuls of beads, beans, rice, or seeds in each tube.
4. Put the lids back on the tubes. Tape down each lid.

Play a favorite song and keep its rhythm by shaking the instruments. For a different sound, gently hit one rhythm tube against the other. Add more beads, beans, rice, or seeds for different sounds.

# Words to Know

**choir** (KWIRE)—a group of people who sing together

**commercial** (kuh-MUR-shuhl)—a notice on TV or on the radio that calls attention to a product or to an event

**equipment** (i-KWIP-muhnt)—the tools and machines needed for an activity

**orchestra** (OR-kess-truh)—a large group of musicians who perform together; orchestras have mostly stringed instruments such as violins.

**professional** (pruh-FESH-uh-nuhl)—getting paid for doing something; professional musicians are paid to perform.

**rhythm** (RITH-uhm)—a regular beat in music

# Read More

**Lee, Barbara.** *Working in Music.* Exploring Careers. Minneapolis: Lerner, 1996.

**Schomp, Virginia.** *If You Were a Musician.* New York: Benchmark Books, 2000.

# Internet Sites

**BLS Career Information**
http://stats.bls.gov/k12/html/edu_over.htm

**The Music Room**
http://www.empire.k12.ca.us/capistrano/Mike/capmusic/home%20page/themusic.htm

**Rock and Roll Hall of Fame and Museum**
http://www.rockhall.com

# Index